The Tree Talks Back

Pictures (all of them) by Esa

Words (most of them) by Bill Grigsby

No egrets Publishing is a registered tirademark, something to do with the last-minute name change from 'No regrets,' perhaps.

© 2015   No egrets Publishing

Esa Grigsby and Bill Grigsby

All rights reserved, reproduction of any portion of this book is prohibited without express written consent of the authors.

ISBN-13: 978-0-9973537-0-9

Library of Congress Control Number: 2016903588

To my Parents, Maria and Bill, and to Giulia, Anna, and Lilah all of whom were ready and willing to read, watch, listen to, observe, eat, touch or otherwise smell any of my current "projects". I owe ya one (or more, each will be evaluated on a case-to-case basis).

To the memory of Fred Johnson, whose extensive knowledge of tropical flora was perhaps surpassed only by his passion for sharing it.

"I think that I shall never see,
a poem lovely as a tree."

Joyce Kilmer, 1913

"How do you tell the difference between
a dogwood and a maple tree?
By the bark."

Esa, circa 1999

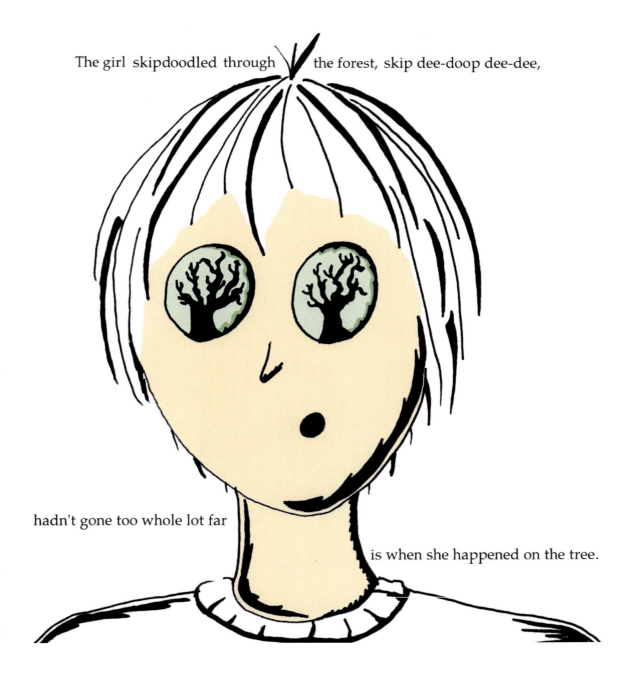

The girl skipdoodled through the forest, skip dee-doop dee-dee,

hadn't gone too whole lot far

is when she happened on the tree.

Biggest tree she ever saw,
craned her neck and dropped her jaw.

*Now with jaw-dropping capability!!!

Everywhere she looked
was branches, branches
draped with leaves,

some with hair or barbs or ribs
and some as big as babies' bibs.

The trunk was gray and smooth
and roots meandered out
like lizards' tails. No! Rocket fins!
Or shell-less snails,

and then plunged down
into the ground
(like roots is s'posed to do,
I've found).

And hangin' from those leafy branches wha'd she find?
    Well you should know—

Flowers?
    No (good guess though),
        but fruit of every kind.

Every kind's a whole lot more
than peaches, pears and plums,
but namin' them all seems like, well,
like countin' leaves when autumn comes.

How big a tree? She couldn't see
the other side, although she tried.

It was lunch and it was red.
"No thank you apple."
She reached for an orange instead.

And as she peeled she said "oh my,"
and looked around, what did she see?

"This tree," said she, "this canopy,
is full of fruit, from where I be.
There's mangos, cherries, lemons, pears,
some with spikes n'stripes n'hair,
guava, melons, breadfruit, plums"
(so watch the skies 'case a big wind comes,
although she wouldn't mind the plums ...),
"think I'm gonna get me some."
But which and where?

"We know it's a snake and don't take our fruit," said the monkey,
torn between snooty and grumpy,
"we need what this tree grows, if it snows, if the wind blows,
if clouds keep their water, the heat gets much hotter or drier
or heaven forbid there's a fire,
well, what will we eat?"

"How sweet! But I won't take too many,"
she said and then "saaay," as she tilted her head
and she saw it, the top of the tree, she barely could see
through a hole in the canopy,
only in books had she seen—
a speckle of purple, framed in green,
"isn't that," she squinted, "a *mangosteen??*"

Yes it was, indeed. "But whyzit here?
Those things grow in Asia."
"We know that, my dear," said the monkey
(leaning towards grumpy).
"Well I've got to have it," she said.

"Well okay, then grab it dag nabbit,
but pleeeease," screeched the parrot, "this isn't your feast,
leave the rest for the jungle and all of us beasts
like the monkeys, apes, rabbits and bats and yes,
even the rats, and the squirrels, ants and penguins,
you hear, silly girl?"

She said "Penguins? In jungles? Absurd! Why whoever heard??"

"Why not? It's a bird," un-convinced the red parrot, "Go choose yer fruit," said a ferret, "climb up to the top, don't stop, pick it clean, leav'er green, mosey off to your shop or whatever you cawl that box, that nest on the ground where you live near that, that . . . . ."

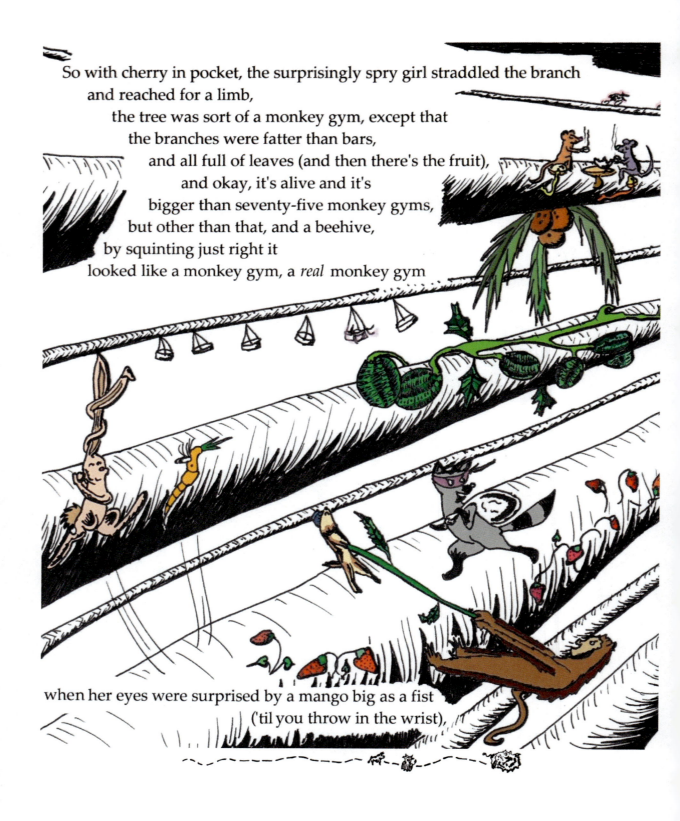

Nor could the monkey or parrot, not even the ferret they watched her grab this and then that and then balance some fruits on her head, like a hat,

'course a slippery few went kersplicketysplat cuzza where she was
    at--real high as she clumbed her way
        up toward the sky through the shade of the tree
        that would whisper when breezes would tickle the leaves
   and then whisk over boughs,
twigs, branches and cows that were lost in the forest.

And she took off her socks and filled those, and she sandwiched blueberries between all her toes, afterthought about
storing a grape in her nose
(which woulda worked better than using her elbows . . .).

"Don't forget," said the monkey (who'd settled on snooty),
"You came for the mangosteen, not *tutti frutti*,
I feel it's my duty to tell you, your pockets, well,
how can I say it?

They're leaking, your blousey is melting, the tree limbs are creaking,
and your shower of fruit has stirred up the ants on the ground,
who are breaking their lines!
And in between fruit bombs some ask
'is the end of the world far behind??'"

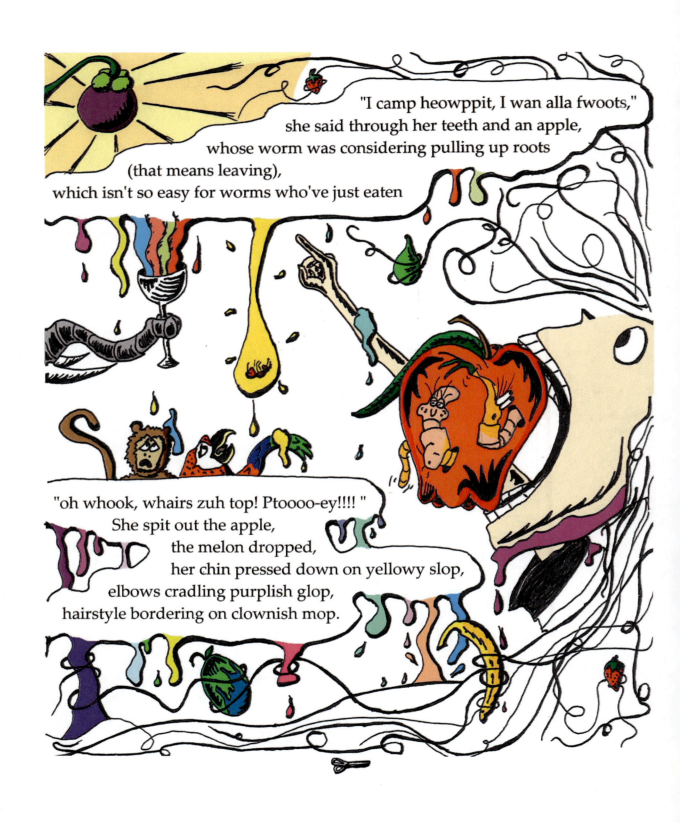

"Three branches til the tip-top tree,
there's the only fruit for me!"

Purple as the iris' tongue
that greets the closing scissors
hung the mangosteen she'd almost won,
velvet dark on golden sun,
three more branches, two then one.

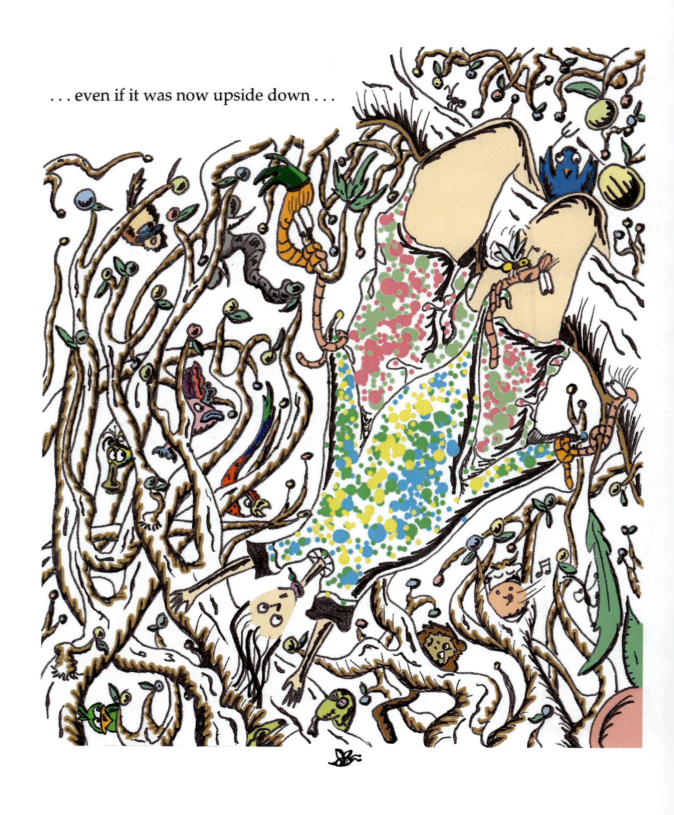
. . . even if it was now upside down . . .

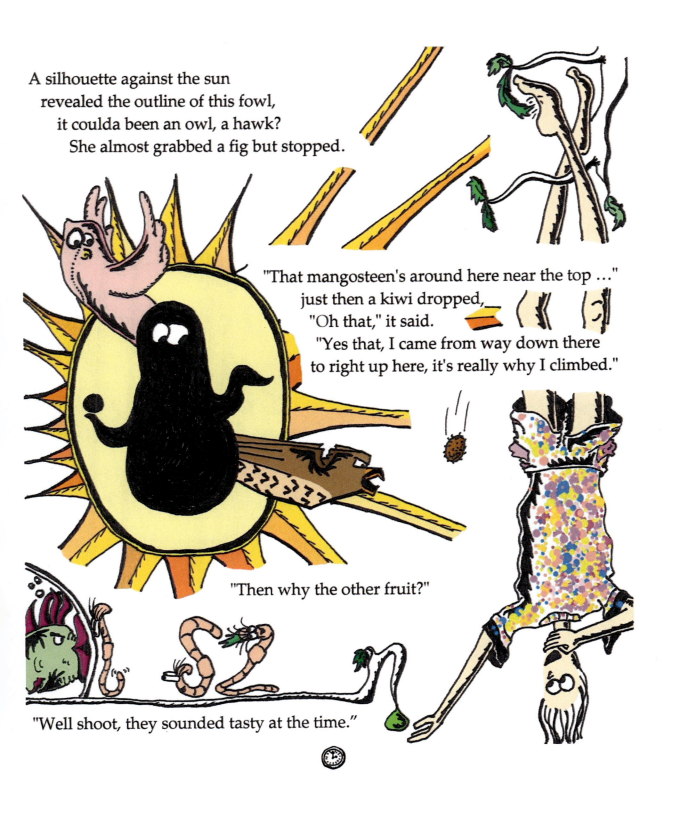

The time!! She thought, she cleared her throat, "Curious Bird, your look is blurred through squinty eyes, but have you seen my purple prize? It must be almost half past five, that's nearly six!"

Oh, you mean this!"
And there it was, the mangosteen, distressed onlookers all around who watched the girl (still upside down) say "Can you stretch your wing? My hand won't reach."

"I am," it squeeched, "a bird, I've stretched my wing, but as I cannot fly I'll try and fling *your* precious mangosteen."

"Why thank you," said the girl, "good night, and anyway, whoever heard of wing-ed birds in tops of trees who can't take flight? Hey wait! This mangosteen—is that . . . *a bite??*"

The sun behind a cloud, she tried, she squinted hard with both her eyes, and finally glimpsed the mystery bird who'd hurled her way a purpled prize . . .

"A penguin? In a tree?? That cannot be!!"

That's when she slipped, she lost her grip.
It seemed to her the trip back down,
bouncing through the leafy crown
went pretty quick. Next thing she knew
she's on the ground, lying down in sticky goo,
staring up at yellow beak-ed you-know-who ...

"Next time," the parrot squawked,
"I'll get your fruit if you
make up your mind, to be so kind
to take the one or two you want and leave the rest behind."

But the girl dared not go back.
She wasn't scared—it wasn't that.
She just thought every fruit should have a tree.
And penguins, should live closer, to the sea.

Esa lives and draws in Portland, Oregon, and has been drawing since way before even this early draft:

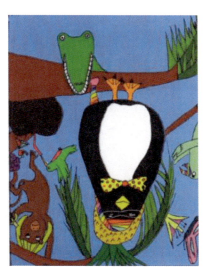

Bill and wife Maria live and work in Eastern Oregon. Late in the evenings, when their three girls were much younger, he would sleep and tell bedtime stories (often at the same time).

For the understory, visit www.thetreetalksback.com

 No egrets Publishing

Made in the USA
Middletown, DE
23 November 2024

64608678R00022